CHICAGO PUBLIC LIBRARY

R00942 14772

YO-CBR-458

Serenity!

Serenity!

Living The Serenity Prayer

by

ig

For DIANE —
positively

TATROE

THE CHICAGO PUBLIC LIBRARY
SOCIAL SCIENCES AND HISTORY DIVISION

FORM 19

Copyright ©1993 by Art Fettig
All rights reserved, including the right of
reproduction in whole or part, in any form

GROWTH UNLIMITED INC.

Dedicated to creating positive living concepts

Art Fettig, President
36 Fairview, Battle Creek, Michigan 49017
Phone 1-800-441-7676 or (616) 965-2229
FAX: (616) 965-4522

Growth Unlimited books are available at quantity discounts with bulk
purchase for educational, business or sales promotional use. For
information, please contact Special Sales Dept., Growth Unlimited
Inc., 36 Fairview, Battle Creek, MI 49017, (616) 965-2229

Manufactured in the United States of America

Design, Layout and
Typesetting
by

Rio Rancho
COMPUTER SERVICES

320 Asbury Rd. NE
Rio Rancho, NM 87124
(505) 892-7226

Library of Congress
Catalog Number 93-077396
Fettig, Art
Serenity! Serenity!

ISBN-0-916927-17-2

Dedication

This book is dedicated to every man, woman and child who ever prayed the Serenity Prayer.

Millions of people in recovery programs all over the world have uttered this prayer, some with desperation, some with hope and others with new joy in their lives.

My hope is that this little book might help to turn that desperation to hope and to joy, for all who read it.

SOCIAL SCIENCES DIVISION
CHICAGO PUBLIC LIBRARY
400 SOUTH STATE STREET
CHICAGO, IL 60605

Foreword

Last night I attended the regular Friday night open meeting of Alcoholics Anonymous here in Battle Creek, Michigan.

They presented me with a brass medallion. On one side it read, "TO THINE OWN SELF BE TRUE" and the words Unity, Service and Recovery. In the center of the coin were the roman numerals XXXII. On the other side of the coin was The Serenity Prayer.

The coin was to commemorate my thirty-two years of continuous sobriety.

The guest speaker was an older fellow, yes, even older than I am, and at one time in his talk he made the remark that he had found serenity.

For thirty-two years now I have been seeking serenity and God knows, I have done a poor job of it. No matter how hard I try I still fail to amass a series of days in which I could say I was truly serene.

It would be presumptuous to suggest that I might try to tell you, the reader, how to live the Serenity Prayer.

Perhaps the real reason for this book is not to teach a person how to live the Serenity Prayer. I guess the real purpose is to challenge the reader to explore the un-limited potential of this prayer.

Somewhere, someone described the different levels of learning. The amateur doesn't know how and he or she doesn't know they don't know. A rookie doesn't know how but somehow realized that he or she doesn't know how and they set out to learn how.

A semi-pro knows how to do something but they don't really know that they know. They are still unsure of their knowledge.

Then a pro not only knows he or she knows. They have confidence and experience.

Now every so often a person reaches a higher level than most of the others. We call these people super-stars in whatever field they perform.

People can become super-stars in most any field. For instance, my daughter, Amy, is getting into the super-star class in quilt making.

Super-stars know. They know they know and more than that, they know why things happen the way they do.

I truly hope that this little book will be of benefit to people no matter what class they might fall into in their quest for Serenity.

If this book simply opens a few eyes to the tremendous power of The Serenity Prayer then my mission will be a success.

The joyous work in writing this book was reward enough for me. Right now, I just might be going through the most challenging time of my life.

There are so many things happening over which I have no control. And each morning I start out the day with The Serenity Prayer.

God, help me see it through this day. Help me in my eternal quest for serenity, I pray.

I wish you serenity, acceptance, courage, wisdom and most of all I wish you love.

GOD

grant me the Serenity to accept the things I cannot change, Courage to change the things I can, and Wisdom to know the difference.

Author Unknown

WHO WROTE THE SERENITY PRAYER? That is a good question and I've been seeking the correct answer to that for some time.

I read one report that said The Serenity Prayer was a prayer for soldiers from the fourteenth century.

Another report from West Germany is as follows. "In the rather dreary hall of a converted hotel, overlooking the Rhine at Koblenz, framed by the flags of famous Prussian regiments, rescued from the Tannenbert memorial, is a tablet inscribed with the following words: "God, give me the detachment to accept those things I cannot alter; the courage to alter those things which I can alter; and the wisdom to distinguish the one from the other." The report states that these words are by Fredrich Otenger, an evangelical pietist of the eighteenth century.

The prayer as we know it today is said to have been written around 1932 by Dr. Reinhold Niebuhr of the Union Theological Seminary in New York City, as the ending to a longer prayer.

In 1934, the doctor's friend and neighbor, Dr. Howard Robbins, asked permission to use this part of the longer prayer in a compilation he was making at the time. It was published in that year in Dr. Robbin's book of prayers.

In 1940 the prayer came to the attention of an early member of A.A. After reading it in an obituary in the New York Herald Tribune, he liked it so well that he called it to the attention of Bill W., one of the founders of A.A. Bill W. felt that it particularly suited the needs of those in A.A. and so cards of the prayer were printed and passed around to members.

When asked about the origin of the prayer, Dr. Niebuhr commented that, "He really didn't know, that it might have been spooking around for years, even centuries..."

Is the prayer just for members of recovery programs? Certainly not. The beauty of this prayer, I find, is that it can fit as a guide to anyone's life. What is life anyway but a series of choices?

Serenity, acceptance, courage, change, wisdom, who could want more in their box of tools to be used in seeking out a happy, productive life?

Like so many other really great prayers or poems where the author has become unknown, I feel that The Serenity Prayer is really something that evolved through the centuries.

Someone comes up with a profound thought. Someone changes a word here, a word there. There is a translation into another language.

Just last week we received a telephone call from someone who asked if my Self Esteem Credo was available in the Spanish language.

Paula, my associate, did not know the answer to that. "I don't know," I had to finally admit. "I suppose that someone has translated it but we do not have a copy at this time," I finally responded.

I know that there is a French translation. And I am certain that when that translation was made that there was some change in meaning.

Perhaps someone will receive that French translation and get the idea to translate my Credo into English.

And who knows how that translation might improve my meager words?

Frankly, I don't think the name of the author is important. I have a belief that when an author really gets in tune with Our Creator that the author sometimes becomes simply a funnel for great inspiration which comes from God.

And so the name of the author, who served as that instrument, is not important. The prayer is important. And The Serenity Prayer has the power to create great change in our lives if we only become open to it.

God help me to live this prayer every day of my life.

The Prayer

THIS MORNING I WAS SITTING IN CHURCH PRAYING and, of course, I started thinking about the Serenity Prayer.

I asked myself, once again, just what are we praying for?

Are we praying for instant wisdom or are we praying for something more reasonable?

Are we hoping for a blinding flash to come and, from that point on, our lives will be filled with wisdom?

If that is our goal in prayer then I am afraid that we are in for disappointment.

I've been in a church on Sunday for most of my life and I have seen thousands and thousands of people in prayer, and in all of that time I have not witnessed one blinding flash among all of those in prayer.

Come to think of it, in the many, many years I have been exposed to this Serenity Prayer, and in association with thousands of others who said The Serenity Prayer, I have never found a person who told about the experience of having a blinding flash after which they were all wise.

I have run into a number of people who believed they were all wise without experiencing the blinding flash, but most of these people had fallen on hard times and the lives they led made me question their wisdom.

Prayer. What is it?

I'm sure everyone has heard the story of the two seamen who were on a raft after their ship had sunk.

The sun was beating down on them and they were out of water.

The one seaman was praying to be saved. They had run out of food and they realized that if they were not rescued within a few hours that they would die. The one seaman prayed aloud, "Oh God, if you save me I will never take another drink of alcohol. And God, if you save me now I will never smoke another cigarette. And, Oh merciful God, if you will just save me, then for the rest of my life I will never..."

And just then the other seaman cried out, "Hold it! I think I see land."

Often prayer is simply a last desperate resort in our misery.

Certainly, when things are going well in our lives our prayers may come to be less fervent.

I like to think of the Serenity Prayer as a daily event.

And with the use of the Serenity Prayer I feel there are personal obligations which go with the prayer.

One of the obligations I feel is that I can no longer go blindly through life with no goal, no plan, no instrument for measuring progress.

Certainly, the Serenity Prayer is often found in the many Twelve Step Recovery Programs.

And so, I feel it reasonable to say that for one thing, it can be classified as a prayer for the recovering.

Call it an instrument for personal survival, if you will.

It is a tool to be used in reconstructing your life.

And I find that it is a tool that must be used daily.

At the office I often use a "Things I have to do" list.

I think it would be a good idea to make a "Things that I cannot possibly do" list.

I can't become seven feet tall. That is, unless I have the misfortune of having one of those steam rollers pass over my body. Then I'd have to change that "can't list" to read, I cannot become seven feet tall and survive.

I can't be thirty years old again . . . or forty or fifty or even sixty.

With a proper diet and the right exercise I am certain that I can feel a whole lot younger than I feel today, but chronologically I cannot turn back the clock which measures my actual age.

And so I have determined that I must do more than simply pray this marvelous prayer each morning to expect the results I pray for. I have to cooperate with God if I expect results.

Today I plan to set some goals for my troublesome life.

Today I hope to identify the various areas in which I hope to improve.

There is more to life than surviving. There is enjoying and thriving and sharing, and loving too, and those are some of the areas that I will think about today.

I'm not a great one for lists but I think I will make a few lists covering the areas in which I hope to grow.

Perhaps you'd care to stop right now and spend some time with your own inventory, your own list.

Then come back and, as the little boy said to the little girl when they were playing doctor, I'll show you mine if you show me yours.

There. That is one of the things that I will put on my list. I'm going to try to raise the quality of my humor. I promise. Well, at least I promise I will try. Who knows, perhaps that is one of those things that I cannot change and in that case I will pray that you are granted the Serenity to accept my humor as it is, or at least be granted the courage to ignore it.

Looking For A Handout

GOD GRANT ME WHAT? THREE THINGS I HAVE DECIDED. I am seeking three Grants, Lord.

Grant #1... God grant me the serenity to accept the things I cannot change.

Grant #2... God grant me the courage to change the things I can change.

Grant #3... God grant me the wisdom to know the difference.

God grant me... Don't sell me these things. Don't loan them to me. I want an outright grant. I don't want you to give me something that I must earn or work off in time. I am praying for an outright grant—no strings attached.

I didn't say "God fax me..."

Not, "God mail me..."

Not, "God play for me or sing to me..."

Just "God grant me," I am looking for an outright hand out, God.

I want the Serenity to accept...

The Courage to change...

But is courage enough? What about action? What about persistence?

Am I expecting God to grant me success or does asking for courage acknowledge the fact that this job of seeking a good life requires a daily, continuing, all out effort on my behalf?

By this Serenity Prayer, am I acknowledging the fact that success is really an inside job—not something which comes with just a prayer or by obtaining a grant?

Just what is it we are seeking from God with this Serenity Prayer? Are we seeking wealth, success, happiness?

No. We are seeking just three things. First, Serenity to accept the things we cannot change.

Second, we seek the courage to change the things we can.

And Third, that wisdom to know the difference.

When I first began my examination of this prayer I somehow believed that it was a marvelous, all-purpose fixer-upper that would somehow, magically solve all things for all people if they would only learn to use the prayer properly.

Now that I have put the words into what seems to be their proper category, I've come to the conclusion that the prayer was never intended as a cure-all for people with problems.

The prayer is a fantastic device for helping people sort out the problems and challenges which face them each day.

Oh Lord, help me to figure out which pile to toss these seemingly impossible messes into so that I might get on with the job of attempting to satisfy or rectify or deal with them, one at a time, in a sane and sober manner.

Lord, I have two piles. One for things I can change and one for things I cannot change.

Lord, give me the wisdom to put these problems in the right pile, because, Lord, if I put them into the wrong pile then I just might spend the rest of my life trying to change something which just cannot be changed and that will be a real waste.

Wisdom, Lord, that is what I need. A good stiff shot or a giant bundle of wisdom. I don't know for certain just what form wisdom comes in because, honestly, I have not been blessed with a lot of it in my life so far.

Really, God, I am ready for a real load of wisdom in my life right now, so lay it on me.

Courage, Serenity, Acceptance, Change, sure Lord, I need a lot of all of those blessings but most of all and first of all, I need a real load of wisdom so that I can put all of those other wonderful things you will grant me to work, properly.

Serenity

Serenity—That little bit
I've got of it
Makes me want
A whole lot more of it.
Life's a piece of cake
when we let go
And let God in.
Serenity—That joy
Of having the gift
Of God's love in our lives.

Serenity and Love

WHAT WOULD YOU SAY IF I TOLD YOU that all addictions are caused by the misdirected quest for serenity?

People want to feel mellow and they sometimes succeed temporarily with alcohol and other drugs, with overeating, or gambling, and they try to achieve and to retain that mellow feeling in their lives through the use of those outside agents.

The problem is this; serenity is an inside job. Serenity comes when you are at peace with yourself, with others and with the world. It does not depend on sex or power or wealth.

In my book *Love is the Target*, I expressed my belief that our whole purpose in life should be to love God, to love ourselves, and to love others. This one truth is prevalent in most religions. It can be found in both the old and the new testaments of the Bible. Jesus once explained it to a lawyer. "You shall love the Lord thy God with your whole heart and soul and you shall love thy neighbor as thyself."

Love God, love yourself, love your neighbor, that is it!

Love is the Target!

May I suggest to you that love is the key to serenity? May I also suggest that the reason for most of our addictions and for the problems in our lives is the fact that we have become most unloving in the way we think and the way we live?

Now am I saying that it is easy to live a life of unconditional love today? Of course not. I am saying that I believe that the real key to serenity is loving and if we seek serenity we are a lot better off seeking it from love than from a bottle or a fist full of pills.

In one of my children's books, my characters, the Three Robots: Pos, Semi-Pos and Neg, teach an old derelict about love and loving.

In my children's series, I try to teach children and their parents truths and positive values as they follow the adventures of my robots.

Our derelict character hates everyone and everything. He is especially bitter because nobody seems to love him. He is one of those characters that go through life crying out, "Love me, love me, you lousy bunch of scumballs."

Of course nobody loves him. Our robots explain to this poor old man that love does not work that way. First he must become loveable. He must clean up himself and his act. After becoming loveable, he must then learn to love himself. When that is accomplished, they help him learn to love others and finally, after becoming loveable, loving himself and loving others; only then is he loved in return.

Perhaps you remember that late great singer, Nat King Cole. If not, then you've probably heard of his daughter, Natalie Cole. One of Nat's greatest song hits was a tune called *Nature Boy*. One of the lines of that song sticks in my mind. It says, "The greatest thing you'll ever learn is just to love and be loved in return."

That is the lesson our Three Robots teach this old man and at the end of the story, the old man has really discovered the lesson of loving.

I just realized what that look on the old man's face represents. It is serenity. Certainly the old man is happy with his new friends and with his newfound knowledge, but there is something beyond that. The old man has found peace with himself and with the world. He has experienced a new inner peace through loving. Serenity.

Oh God, grant me serenity, make me a loving person.

Ticked Off Serenity

THE OTHER DAY A FRIEND OF MINE NAMED CEZAR visited me and as I was explaining something to him I made the remark, "That really ticks me off." (Actually I said something very close to that.)

Cezar looked me straight in the eye and said, "Lately, Art, everything ticks you off."

Cezar has been my good friend for many, many years. It must be over twenty-five years now that Cezar has been telling me the truth, regardless of how badly it might hurt. He does it as gently as possible, but still he does it.

At least, Cezar tells me the truth as he perceives it. I often disagree with him but on far too many occasions he is right on target.

He didn't say a heck of a lot more that day. I guess he knew when he'd made his point and he withdrew gracefully.

I've thought a lot about what Cezar said, and since then I must admit that a lot of things and a lot of people have been disturbing me recently. In fact, you might say that they really tick me off. (Or something quite like that.)

Oh, sure, I could blame it all on current events and say that, just maybe I am not my old, sweet, smiling, loveable self, but the sad fact is that I am never sweet and smiling and all that loveable either, ever.

It isn't that I am mean and hateful and all that, but I really do leave a lot to be desired in the sweet and loveable category.

So why am I ticked off at the world lately?

Well, I'm on a diet for one thing. That never sweetens me up no matter how well it is going.

My back is acting up and I have a lot of pain in my low back lately.

My wife, Ruthie, has been sick for over two months in a row and that breaks my heart every day because there is so little that I seem able to do for her.

Oh, I could go on with a lot more little things that are nagging at me, but as I see what I've written it suddenly dawns on me that I am not really living The Serenity Prayer.

People and events shouldn't be ticking me off. Everything that happens has its rightful place in The Serenity Prayer.

Oh God, grant me the serenity—that explains that lack of a smile on my face, I am suffering from an acute shortage of serenity.

Grant me the serenity to accept those things I cannot change.

I cannot expect to take this excess weight off without some painful effort but why must I make it painful for others by my sour disposition?

Sweeten up, guy. Smile through that pain.

God help me to accept the fact that I have low back problems. I should either go to a surgeon and let him hack away at me or else do my exercises. I must get rid of that excess weight and, for the time being, grin and bear it.

Quit getting ticked off at people and things!

About Ruthie? Accept the fact that Ruthie now has cancer of the liver and there is really no miracle cure.

Just thank God each day for the miracle you've already received, an extra year with Ruthie. And what a wonderful year, with ten wonderful vacations together.

Now accept one day at a time and make your best effort to bring just a bit of joy into Ruthie's life to ease her pain, if for just a moment.

Getting ticked off at things and people won't help you with Ruthie at all.

God, grant me the courage to change the things I can.

So I can't change my weight today, but I can change it over a period of time. I can't change the fact that I have an old back which was never all that good to begin with. But I can do my exercises and keep on working on that diet to get rid of that fat gut which puts all that extra strain on my back.

I can't change the fact that Ruthie has cancer of the liver and that the doctors say it is terminal, but I can dedicate each day to doing the things I can to make her days and nights more bearable.

I guess that God sent Cezar over to me the other day to share His wisdom with me.

Wisdom, that is what I need a lot more of these days. The wisdom to sort out the things that have been ticking me off and the courage to face those things with the continuing help of my Creator.

Serenity And Death

AT THE TIME I WRITE THIS, MY WIFE, RUTHIE, is at home suffering badly. There are so many things I would like to do to relieve her pain but I do not know where to begin.

My daughter, Nancy, who came home from California just the other day to visit with her mom, called the doctor and he prescribed a stronger pain killer and now Ruthie is upstairs sleeping.

Ruthie has cancer of the liver and now the cancer has spread to the bones in her back. It is extremely painful and there just are no answers that will help Ruthie's condition. Not now. Not yet. After spending billions of dollars on cancer research they still have no answers for my Ruthie.

It was eight years, one month ago that we first discovered that Ruthie had breast cancer. For eight years now we have been living through one test after another and now it has come to this. There are no more answers.

I certainly hope that I am wrong but I do not expect Ruthie to live more than a few more weeks or possibly a few more months and when I see her suffer so, I hope that it will be much sooner than later.

For thirty-eight years we have been together as man and wife. We've never left each other. We've stuck it out through so much and now I must come to the acceptance that she will soon be leaving. I now love her more than ever.

It is such a helpless feeling, knowing that there is really nothing that can be done.

This morning I took her a CD of the best music of Lloyd Weber. *Memories* is her favorite song and I put it on to play and she listened for a few seconds and then she left the room. She went into our living room and sat in a chair and she tried bravely to sing the words of the song but the pain she was enduring was too great.

Oh God, it hurts so badly to see someone you love that much suffer so. A few moments later, Nancy called the doctor at his home and asked if he could prescribe a different pain pill because the one she was using certainly was not providing the relief she needed.

My mind keeps filling up with thoughts of the future. What will it be like to be alone for the first time in my life?

What will it be like to live in our huge house alone? To eat alone, to go to church on Sundays alone, to travel to those wonderful places I sometimes visit, alone.

Is serenity the absence of pain? I wonder. If serenity is the absence of pain then God grant Ruthie serenity right now, this instant.

Yesterday Ruthie made the comment that the pain she had endured in the past few months must certainly make up for all the things she had done wrong in her lifetime and I guess she is right.

What did she do wrong, except perhaps marry me?

I'm sitting here typing this manuscript in my office, less than a city block from our home and every hour or so I go home and check up on Ruthie. She is still sleeping, thank God. At least, I believe that when she sleeps she is not consciously aware of that pain.

I keep praying that Ruthie will wake up tomorrow morning and that she will be cured and that we can go on for another year and then another and another, but we have already experienced the miracle of eight more years together since that cancer was first discovered.

A little over a year ago I felt that I was losing my Ruthie and then we did experience our miracle. She found a nutritionalist who put her on a new track and she improved tremendously.

Ruthie looked ten or even twenty years younger and we were able to take a dozen wonderful vacations together.

Then in September she discovered that the spots were back on her liver and all of the other tests for cancer indicated that things were not right.

She's been really sick for over three months now and God how she has suffered. Please God, give us a miracle, right now before she suffers any more and if you cannot grant us a healing then grant her rest, amen.

Acceptance

I want to change it all,

To change it all, God,

Especially the unchangeable,

That is the hurdle.

Certainly, that is impossible God,

You know it and I know it,

But knowing is not enough.

Not near enough.

I must accept it and acceptance

Is my most lacking,

And most required trait.

Oh God, give me acceptance.

A.S.A.P.

Editor's Note

The cancer in Ruthie's body spread throughout her liver, then to her spine, her chest, and finally, to her brain.

After a series of struggles both in and out of the hospital, Ruthie finally died on the afternoon of June 26, 1993.

May she rest in peace.

Sculptor, Artist And Acceptor

WHAT IS THAT SAYING ABOUT WHEN SOMEONE gives you a lemon you make lemonade? I guess that is it. And when we talk about acceptance we discover that the way we react to that acceptance makes all of the difference in the world.

On September 13, 1501, a sculptor named Michelangelo Buonarroti accepted a challenge that no other sculptor at the time would accept.

A previous sculptor had ruined a huge piece of marble in the city of Florence, Italy, and the mutilated block had remained in possession of the city for many years.

For one thing, the marble had been blocked out in an unconventional slab that was long and thin. Not a piece that would lend itself to most of the sculpture of that time. Furthermore, the previous sculptor who had abandoned his project had carved a deep triangular gash near the base.

Although many artists had considered the project, they all came to the conclusion that making something worthwhile out of this ruined piece of marble was impossible.

And now, Michelangelo took his chisel in hand and began his work.

Two and a half years later he completed his project and they called in all of the critics of Europe. They declared it a masterpiece.

From this ruined piece of marble, Michelangelo had created the statue of David, the giant killer, as he faced his enemy, Goliath.

Today, in Florence, Italy, tourists line up for hours to view the masterpiece. Many consider it the greatest piece of sculpture ever created.

There is a story about this work. It is said that once a critic approached Michelangelo and asked him, "How, Michelangelo, could you create this wonder from a piece of marble which had been mutilated?" And Michelangelo replied, "It was already there. When I first saw the marble I saw David standing there in all of his splendor. All I had to do was knock away all of the marble which did not belong there."

And the critic persisted, "What about the flaw?" And Michelangelo replied, "That didn't belong there anyway. That was a place between his legs which had to be taken out anyway."

Michelangelo saw the possibility in what remained of the block of marble, not its flaws.

Certainly, he accepted what there was to work with in this project and he used every flaw, every challenge as a stepping stone to perfection.

Later, some other jealous artists persuaded Pope Julius to assign to Michelangelo the task of painting the ceiling of the Pope's private chapel called the Sistine.

Michelangelo insisted that painting was not his art, that he was a sculptor, however the Pope insisted and finally, Michelangelo settled down to the enormous project. The ceiling covered an area of some 10,000 square feet that had to be covered with pictures. Michelangelo spent the next four years practically a prisoner, slaving away on his back creating what many consider the greatest work of art of all time.

Not a painter? Painting not his art? And painting a ceiling, yet, in fresco, a technique which required the grinding of colors mixed with water, not oil, and then laying them on wet plaster. As the plaster dried, the color was set forever in the lime. This form required that the artist work at top speed before the plaster dried.

Acceptance? Certainly Michelangelo accepted the order from Pope Julius to paint the ceiling of his chapel and then he got caught up in the project to the extent that he worked every day for long hours until finally the Pope insisted that the project had been completed. Michelangelo was not yet satisfied with his work and the Pope finally threatened to have him thrown out if he did not stop.

And so, once again, the critics were called in to see the work.

There are 343 major figures in the ceiling. Critics still agree that this work is not simply a masterpiece but a whole series of masterpieces brought together in one work.

The story of Michelangelo keeps coming back to me and I think it is a story that exemplifies one living the Serenity Prayer.

Lord, grant me the serenity to accept the things I cannot change.

Michelangelo totally surrendered to the obstacles that were presented to him in these projects. And after this surrender he went to work with a passion to overcome those things which could be changed.

What courage! What wisdom! What total dedication and persistence!

What can we learn from Michelangelo? We can learn that simply having a talent is not enough. Talent requires discipline and hard work and persistence, combined with courage and whatever wisdom we can gain.

As Michelangelo is reported to have said, the masterpiece is already there. All we have to do is knock off those pieces of marble which do not belong there. Some of us must get that chip off our shoulder.

We are all masterpieces, you and I. Our challenge is to rid ourselves of the flaws and imperfections which do not belong there.

That is our challenge.

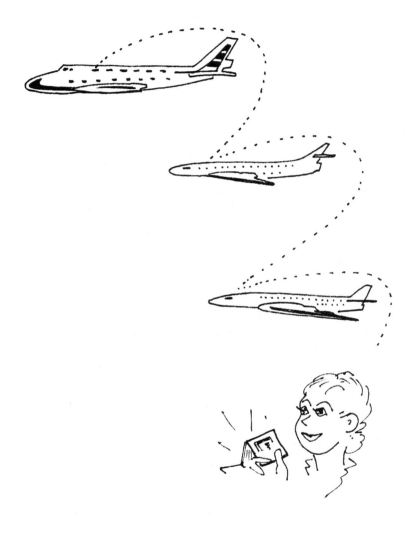

Accepting The Bumps

YESTERDAY OUR DAUGHTER, AMY, FLEW IN from her home in San Diego to visit us for Christmas.

She saved a small bundle by flying Continental Airlines.

Our nearest airport is Kalamazoo, Michigan, and the route she flew was San Diego to Denver to Cleveland to Kalamazoo.

The flights were overbooked and at both San Diego and Denver she volunteered to give up her seat and wait for a later flight. In return for this the airline usually gives you a round trip ticket for any of their trips in the continental U.S.

In both instances, as it turned out, they did not need to take her up on her offer, however, as a gesture of their appreciation they upgraded her to a first class seat.

Amy is great at volunteering for a bump off a plane and I predict that before she arrives back in San Diego on this trip that she will take a bump, suffer a few hour delay and arrive home with another ticket for a free flight in her purse. And I'll make another prediction. I believe that when she takes that free flight, she will accept another bump along the way and earn still another free flight.

How does she accomplish this? She simply positions herself for opportunity.

When she checks in for a flight she lets the attendants know that she is willing to take a bump for a free flight. When they find they need a seat because they have overbooked they simply call on her.

I've seen times when she took a bump and because of delays she arrived at her final destination at the same time she had previously planned.

Now for just a moment I'd like you to join me as we observe the other people who were scheduled for that same flight. Often a few of them arrive at the last moment. They have booked a seat perhaps and they expect to get on that plane but when they check in they are told that the plane is overbooked and that their seat has been reassigned to someone else.

What is their reaction? Do they smile and say, "OK, but it will cost you a free ticket."? Hardly. Often their reaction is anger and hostility.

I've heard them scream at the attendant, "What kind of an airline are you running, anyway, overbooking flights?"

You can just see the anxiety mounting.

Stress raises its ugly head.

There is tension.

The next few moments seem like hours. The people involved start to imagine that their whole lives will go down the drain if they do not board that flight immediately.

They want a seat and they want it now.

I'm thinking about acceptance and serenity right now.

My daughter, Amy, accepts the fact that all of the airlines out of San Diego often overbook their flights. It is a fact of life. And she knows that quite often there is another flight to her destination just a few hours later.

Amy lives just a few minutes drive from the San Diego airport.

If she takes a bump in San Diego she can actually hop into her car and be about her business for an hour or two or whatever.

Amy accepts reality and uses it to her advantage.

How did she get to this point of acceptance when it comes to air travel?

When Amy was a young girl I had the good fortune of qualifying for free travel on Air Canada Airlines for my whole family.

Each summer I would take two of our four children to Europe for a couple of weeks of travel.

We would drive across the US-Canada border at Windsor, Ontario and board a flight to Toronto.

My passes were on a stand-by basis so we could not book definite reservations on a flight, but we did have pretty good priority on our passes.

I'd obtain airline passes and then I would request a fist full of train passes too. I worked for a railroad but I also represented Air Canada in a minor way which qualified me for free air travel.

As we planned our trip we realized that flexibility was essential. We had to take things as they came to us and so we did not set a definite agenda.

Perhaps we set our sights on Paris and we put in for stand-by reservations on a flight to Paris. When we checked in we'd ask how our chances were to get on that flight. Many times the flights went without a hitch just as we'd hoped, but there were times that flights were crowded and we didn't get our first choice.

Fortunately, I taught the children the importance of packing a bag that they could carry onto a plane or a train and so we did not have the problem of checking baggage.

When the flight we hoped for was booked, we simply went over to the Departure board and picked out another destination. Paris, Zurich, Frankfort, London, Amsterdam, Copenhagen, they really made no real difference to us, they were all capable of providing us with a memorable vacation.

We seldom had to stay in Toronto more than a couple of hours until we caught a flight to Europe and were on our way to an exciting adventure.

Perhaps these experiences played some part in creating Amy's relaxed attitude toward travel.

With my working schedule, most of the time I must arrive at a certain place at a certain time to work and so delays could prove to be very costly to me. I am an impatient traveler. I dread delays or cancelled flights.

But now and then, on my trip home I find that our plane is overbooked and they ask for volunteers to take a later flight. They offer free tickets, of course, and I think about my daughter Amy. I raise my hand and walk to the door. It helps to improve my perspective about flying.

I certainly cannot change the fact that today, airlines often overbook their flights.

That is something I cannot change. They simply will not change their practice just for me. And so I pray for the Serenity to accept this situation which I cannot change, however I recognize the fact that I can change my attitude toward this situation. Instead of it being an irritant I turn it into an opportunity.

I take a bump and arrive home just a few hours later with a round trip ticket in my pocket and a smile on my face.

And if you are like me you believed that our children are supposed to learn from us. And, hopefully, our children do learn from us, however we must also accept the fact that what goes around comes around.

Often the lessons we teach our children somehow elude us as we grow older and we must be open to wisdom from whatever source it is offered.

We teach our children, yes. But there is so much we can learn from our children, too, if we simply open ourselves to growth.

There are some wonderful benefits to be derived from this serenity business if we only allow ourselves to learn.

J'll Pass You Later...

A FRIEND OF MINE TEACHES A DEFENSIVE DRIVING program. His wife claims that he had to take the course a dozen times himself before he really caught on and by then he was so well known to the people who taught the course that they finally took him on as an instructor.

We were out driving in the Atlanta area and traffic was as thick as Alabama mud. After a while I realized that my friend was easing back and letting the heavy build up of traffic pull ahead of him.

After a few moments of this I suddenly realized that we were all alone there on the highway. Ahead a couple of hundred yards you could see the pile up of traffic, but where we were there was no traffic beside us nor ahead or behind us for a few hundred yards.

"Art," he explained to me, "there are islands of clear space in nearly every traffic pattern if you learn to look for them. You simply have to ease up on the gas pedal and let the heavy traffic go around you and in a minute or so you find you have a nice clear space all to yourself."

We drove along like that and every minute or so a car would come charging up from behind us and pass us.

"That's what we call a Charger," my friend explained, and as the car went charging by my friend just smiled at the other driver and said out loud, "I'll pass you later."

Then he turned to me and explained, "Those Chargers really aren't going anywhere. They just go up ahead and get jammed up with that pack."

The other day I was driving into Chicago and I was up there with the pack and I noticed that in the three lane traffic we were in I was totally surrounded by big, heavy, diesel burning, tractor-trailers. There were dozens of them all around me and we were all charging ahead.

It was really stressful. I realized how tense my body was and there was a real mean scowl on my face.

I eased back on the gas pedal and in a moment I noticed that the tractors behind me started pulling into other lanes to go around me.

In about a minute or perhaps two I found myself alone in an island of tranquility. Or could you call it an island of serenity?

There was no traffic on my right or on my left or in front or behind me for a couple of hundred yards.

I just kept maintaining a speed that would keep me a few hundred yards behind the pack.

A semi came charging up behind me on the left lane and as he passed I just smiled. I guess you might call it more of a knowing grin. "I'll pass you later," I said.

As I drove along I felt the pressure easing and the stress leaving my body. My scowl was replaced with a pleasant smile.

I started wondering as I drove along if, just maybe, there are these islands of serenity available in other places too besides our highways.

I'll bet by slightly changing our schedules we could avoid those crowds at 12 noon in the restaurants.

Perhaps if I thought a bit more about other people's schedules I could arrange my contact to catch them at a better time too.

Just maybe I could find a lot more serenity every day in my life if I just thought about things a bit more, if I kept my eyes open looking for those Serenity Islands.

I'll bet you they are there just waiting for us. Anyway, I'm going to look and I'm going to expect to find a lot of them.

Begrudging Acceptance

HAVE YOU EVER STARED A PROVEN FACT RIGHT IN THE EYE and refused to accept it?

Once in a great while you might read about some great scientist or inventor or explorer who refused to accept something that was presented as pure fact and after many years of persistence and hard work they proved that the fact, believed by all others, was not a fact at all but simply a belief which was not true.

The stories I listened to as a child told me that everyone at the time of Columbus believed that the world was flat. That if you sailed out too far you would fall off the end of the earth.

Columbus, it was said, believed the world was round and he had the courage and the persistence to go out and prove it. I guess that the real fact is that many people believed the world was round but, nevertheless, it makes a heck of a story, especially for children.

My problem is that I often look at facts which are true and I simply refuse to accept them.

The other night I was scheduled to make a video tape of my talk titled, *Love is the Target*. We had the banquet room arranged, a great audience scheduled, a marvelous video photographer was hired and all I had to do was get prettied up and get my speech in order.

It was in the process of getting prettied up that I encountered a cold, hard fact and I stared it right in the eye and denied it. The fact is that I have a rather obnoxious pot belly. It sticks out thaaaaat far.

For three weeks before the video taping I went into serious training for the assignment. I dieted faithfully; I exercised; and I lost weight too. In fact, in three weeks I lost eight pounds. That is a fact. Also a fact is that my pot belly was of the thirty to forty pound variety.

I have this really nice, partially silk, herringbone type sports jacket. I had planned to wear it for the taping and each week I would try it on and, although I could button the jacket in front, it strongly resisted the idea.

On the morning of the taping I donned the jacket, took a deep breath and buttoned her up. Then I walked bravely to a full-length mirror to see how I'd look on television. "Not bad!" I said to myself. "Not bad at all." This is what is commonly known as denial.

I spun around in front of the mirror a couple of times to get first a front view, then a profile view from the right and the left and again I lied to myself. "I think it will work out just fine."

That morning I bought a Detroit Free Press newspaper, and I noticed that there was a suit and jacket sale at a store just a few miles from the hotel where we were taping our video program.

I slipped a plastic cover over my jacket and decided to head for the banquet hall an hour early, just in case I decided to drop in at the clothing store first.

Somewhere on the interstate highway between Battle Creek and Detroit I came up with the idea of asking for a second opinion. I'd take my jacket into the clothing store, try it on and ask some of the salespeople there what they thought of the fit.

I sought out the friendliest looking salesman I could find and explained my situation. Then I put on the jacket. He took one quick look and said, "It's too tight."

At my request, he called over two other salespeople. "It's too tight," they both agreed.

"Your gut is pushing out so hard on that button that it throws the whole jacket out of place." Then he added, "Let me show you how a jacket should hang on you."

He walked over and took a forty-six long off the rack. Mine was a forty-four long. The jacket looked great on me. "Of course, if you want to call attention to your big gut, then wear the old one," he said.

I took off the new jacket and put the old one on again. "I don't think it's really that bad, do you?" I asked.

They didn't answer.

"Maybe I could just leave the button unbuttoned."

Again, they didn't answer.

Finally I shrugged and said, "OK, I'll take the jacket."

"What about slacks?" the salesman I'd started out with asked.

Somehow he no longer seemed like the friendliest one.

"The slacks?" I asked.

"Yes, the slacks, you've got them pushed down and your gut is hanging over the top of them." The salesman said.

"Oh, you noticed that," I said. "I didn't think anyone would notice."

"Everyone notices," he said.

I bought the slacks he picked out for me to go with the jacket. I needed a new belt too. And I tried on my shirt. Then he showed me how my neck hung over the collar when I buttoned it. I bought a shirt and a tie to go with the new shirt and a hankie to go in the pocket of my new jacket.

I must admit that I looked great when I went in to make that video. There was nothing hanging over. Nothing.

Oh God, grant me the serenity to accept the fact that it will take more than three weeks to get rid of that forty pound gut. And grant me the courage to hang in there. And the wisdom to know when too small is just too small . . . period.

Bumper Cars

BY ACCEPTING THE THINGS WE CANNOT CHANGE we do not mean that we resign ourselves to a life of misery and defeat.

When it comes to problem solving I often imagine myself in an amusement park and I am the driver of one of those Bumper Cars.

Bumper cars have rubber bumper cushions all around them so that you can run into the other bumper cars without visible damage.

Oh, you might give the other driver quite a jolt, especially when you come up from behind without the other driver's knowledge and give that car a real bump.

The beauty of a Bumper Car is that when you run into an obstacle you can just spin the steering wheel and dart off into a new direction.

Then once you get going again you can head once more to your destination.

I've heard it said that once an airplane taxis down the runway and takes off that it is off course for most of the trip to its destination.

Winds blow and other factors enter in, however, the pilot keeps on resetting his sights on the final destination. Of course, today, this can be done automatically, but the fact remains, most of the time the plane is not actually flying directly towards its final target.

Like the driver of that Bumper Car, the pilot or automatic pilot of that plane keeps dealing with outside forces or you might call them problems or obstacles or challenges or whatever. And instead of trying to change those obstacles the driver simply makes adjustments.

The point is that serenity may help us accept the things that we cannot change but it does not necessarily follow that we must lie down like puppy dogs, roll over and play dead.

Life offers us an unlimited number of options and it becomes exciting and wonderful when we learn to look for opportunities for change and daily opportunities for personal growth.

Less Than Meets The Eye

A S AN AUTHOR OF THIRTY-THREE PUBLISHED BOOKS and a countless number of other published articles and such, I am often accused of being a lot more intelligent and profound than I really am.

People often read all sorts of meaning into something that I have written. Of course, I just stand there and love every moment of it.

This often happens to people who write plays or who produce movies too. Critics assign all sorts of profound meaning to things that were not at all in the writer's or the producer's mind at the time of creation.

Now, when it comes to spiritual or inspirational writing one might argue that the writer was merely acting as an instrument of The Holy Spirit.

That I will buy. Many times I have given speeches to large audiences and the feedback from the audience will tell me that everyone in that audience received a different message from what I said.

For instance, I once had the opportunity to speak for an audience of several hundred people. There were students from kindergarten through twelfth grade. There were the students' parents and their teachers. And at the head table were representatives of the Board of Education for our State.

We had a wide range of ages and educational backgrounds.

After my forty-five minute talk the head of the board approached me. "Mr. Fettig," she said. "I have heard you speak before but this is the first time I've sat at a head table while you stood out in front of us and I had the opportunity to observe the audience. Do you realize that you held the absolute attention of every member of that audience for a full forty-five minutes?"

"Yes, I noticed that," I admitted. "Weren't they wonderful."

Before my talk this same woman had tried speaking for this group and within a few seconds the children were stirring and moving around and parents and teachers began talking with one another.

"That was amazing," she continued. "How could you possibly do this?"

"I couldn't do it myself," I told her. "Perhaps you didn't notice it but I said a prayer just before I walked out there to speak."

Frankly, I had looked the audience over beforehand and I decided that no one could hold that audience. I just prayed that I might do the best job possible. At that point I did not really feel responsible for what happened. I felt that I was being used as an instrument of The Holy Spirit and that if I could just get out of the way of my own ego and my own selfishness that I would be alright with that audience.

Now we might not really know who wrote The Serenity Prayer. We do not know the circumstances in which it was written. Perhaps some poor soul had simply gone to the limits of his or her ability to cope with life any longer and in complete surrender had taken a pen or quill in hand and written a plea for help.

And perhaps through the centuries as hundreds and thousands and millions of people have discovered the prayer, each of them heard a different message in that wonderful prayer.

I have discussed this prayer with others and each seems to bring his or her own level of meaning to the prayer.

Sometimes I do not accept their translation and I might silently say to myself, "There is less to this than meets the eye." And then I stand back and say, "God let this prayer be the light in the tunnel or the balm that each person requires at a given moment to find hope and joy."

Courage

Courage— That stuff of which
Heroes and heroine are made.
God, I need a ton of it
And more for what I must soon do.
To change those things I can—
Courage— that will be a start.
The courage to live my life
Twenty-four hours at a time.
The courage to face the next moment,
The next day and, God,
If you will renew that courage
On a daily basis,
Then I can make a good life of it.

Praying For Courage

I N 1952 I WAS A COMBAT RIFLEMAN IN KOREA. One cold early morning in November we were about to go on an attack of a hill that was covered with enemy dead from many hours of fighting.

It was our time to participate in the attack and as we waited on the side of a nearby hill we watched the long line of our G.I. dead and wounded as they were carried by our position.

Before we received the order to move forward I got down on my knees and I prayed to God for courage. Frankly I was terrified at the thought of running through that open area in front of the hill where we were attacked.

The enemy had that area zeroed in with their artillery and their mortar fire and already it had become known as Death Valley.

Just getting through that valley alive was not enough though, because then the fighting became even more fierce.

I prayed at that moment harder than I had ever prayed in my life. Of course, I prayed for survival, too, but most of all I prayed for the courage to do the job which was assigned to me on that attack.

I made it about half way up that hill before I was hit by mortar fire and then all of my prayers were answered.

A medic plugged me up to stop the bleeding and I was evacuated. Now, every day I pray for the courage to confront all of those other problems and challenges that come into my life on a daily basis.

I pray for that courage to change the things that I can.

I pray for the courage to plan. To dream. To try. To persist.

I pray for the courage to change. To overcome defeat or to accept it. I pray for the courage to live with misunderstanding as I try to correct it.

I pray for the courage to face today and to take tomorrow as it comes.

I pray for the courage to stand up for what I believe in my heart.

For the courage to put doing good over personal gain.

I pray for the courage to grow. To live with the pain in my life.

I pray for the courage to do what I must do to make this a better life and a better world.

Yes, God, grant me courage.

To Change

To change, to change,
To rearrange
The circumstances of my life.
To change, Oh God,
change is so frightening,
So threatening, so—soo—
change is so unpredictable—
And yet, God, I know
That change is so essential
To my life and my future
And to my happiness that I pray,
God, Please help me change.

The Courage To Change Those Things Which We Can

SUE SATTERFIELD IS A REAL "SOUTHERN WOMAN." That is the first thing she made clear to us when we met her in Atlanta, Georgia. Georgia Power Company had hired me to do a series of programs for their supervisors and foremen.

My wife, Ruthie, and I first met Richard Satterfield and his wife, Sue, in April and we returned in October for a second session. They were fantastic hosts on the first trip and so we decided to spend a couple of days visiting the beautiful foothills of northern Georgia together.

We visited the Hiawassee Fairgrounds on a Saturday and then in the evening we attended a Country Music Show. We guessed that there were some five thousand people in the packed auditorium. Luckily we found four seats together at the rear of the giant hall. As we walked inside the auditorium I was hit by the hot, stale air. A group was on-stage singing their hearts out and the audience response was really flat.

Sue sat down, sniffed a bit and said out loud for us all to hear, "This air is foul." And, of course, we all agreed. "I'll take care of that!" she said confidently.

Sue stood up and went to the rear of the hall where the fellow from the Lion's Club, the program's sponsor, sat at a table. "This air is foul in here," she said to the man.

He explained that he was alone at the desk and there was simply nothing he could do about the situation. "We've got to open up some of those side doors," Sue said, and again the man explained that he could do nothing about the matter.

"I'll take care of that!" she said, and she walked over to a fellow sitting on a chair at the rear of the hall. "We are going to let some fresh air into this hall," she said. "Will you help me?"

Actually Sue said, "Will you hep me?" However, I am a Yankee and so there is just no credibility to whatever I report as southern talk.

The man at the rear of the hall stood up and joined Sue as she walked over to the side and, with the help of two other men, slid up one of those big steel sliding overhead doors.

You could feel that sweet smelling Georgia mountain air rush into the huge room. A moment later a second door swung up and more air rushed in.

Then Sue walked over to the far side of the hall with her newly enlisted crew and . . . wham! Another door sailed upward and then yet another.

Now she had a great system of cross ventilation going. It was heavenly.

Five thousand people who had been sitting there suffering with the lack of oxygen and whatever other elements people suck out of the air supply, now began to inhale deeply.

It was like magic. The musicians on the stage began to perform better. The crowd really got into the music, now that their survival was no longer in jeopardy. They started in clapping and stompin' and that turned out to be one of the most wonderful Country Shows that we have attended in a long, long time.

After they'd opened the fourth door, Sue calmly walked back to her seat with us and said proudly, "We took care of that."

Can you imagine, five thousand people were willing to just sit and suffer with really stale air and not one of them made an effort to do anything about it? It took a "real Southern woman" named Sue.

Oh how the world needs more people like her. How many times have we all suffered in silence rather than take the necessary action to make this world a little better?

9421477₂

That Old Demon Dis

A FEW YEARS AGO I READ THAT, IN THE UNITED STATES alone, doctors prescribe three billion Valium and one billion Librium to patients each year.

As I understand it, these drugs are used to kill an inner pain. Evidently, a lot of Americans are hurting inside.

Add to the above the billions of sleeping pills that are sold in America each year and you just might come to the conclusion that a lot of people have a lot on their mind that they would prefer to forget.

While drugs might kill that inner pain temporarily, they do not teach people to accept pain and to grow from it, and that is why these physicians must continue to prescribe these "pleasant pills" year after year.

It has been estimated that 80% of all doctor's patient's ills are emotionally related.

Have you noticed that the hot buzzword today is "stress." You see it a lot in ads for non-prescription drugs.

People like to talk a great deal about their "stress." Jobs are now stressful. In California, lawyers are filing thousands of lawsuits claiming that their clients, who have been laid off by employers, are under a great deal of stress because of their unemployment and that they suffered great stress on the job when they were employed. Stress is now compensable under some states Workmen's Compensation Laws.

Life has become "stressful." Doctor's often tell their patients that they suffer from "stress." Kids are now suffering from stress.

Playing in some Little Leagues has become so competitive that the players suffer from "stress."

I'd like to go on record right now in saying that I believe that all of this "stress" stuff is just a lot of hogwash.

It isn't "stress" that is the culprit, it is "distress."

We need stress to survive. Stress is a good thing. Without stress we are not alive. Without stress buildings would crumble, bridges would fall to the ground and people would cease to be.

Distress is our problem and once again that old demon Dis has reared his ugly head.

What we need to get rid of in our lives is not stress, what we need to get rid of is "dis".

My oversize, hernia producing, ten pound unabridged edition of *The Random House Dictionary of the English Language* states that *dis* is "a learned borrowing from Latin meaning 'apart,' 'asunder,' 'away,' 'utterly,' or having a privative, negative or reversing force..."

Dis is a negative or reversing force.

But let us look at the capitalized meaning of this word. Dis is described as the following. "Dis (1): Also called Dis Pater, a god of the underworld identified with Orcus or the Greek god Pluto. (2) the underworld: Orcus Hades."

We are talking about Satan and about hell.

Now what in the world am I bringing up Dis in a book about The Serenity Prayer? I just happened to discover that a lot of the reason we are praying for Serenity is the fact that there is a lot of dis-harmony in our lives. There are a lot of other harmful elements floating around which make us unhappy and miserable too.

So what else did I discover in my oversized dictionary? A lot. I found nearly twelve full pages of words that begin with dis.

In fact, I found many of the best words in the English language that had been turned around and made ugly by putting a dis in front of them.

Let me just name a few of them. I'll give you the word and you put a dis in front of it and see what happens. Able, advantage, agreement, appear, approve, array, belief, comfort, courage, courtesy, credit, ease, enchantment, favor, figure, grace, harmony, honesty, honor...

I think you get the idea.

Now can you see why we ought to make an honest effort to get the Dis out of our lives?

Why don't we both try something today. I'll do mine and you do yours. Go through a giant dictionary and write down all of the dis words that represent the things you dislike the most in others. For instance, dishonesty, disgrace, disbelief. You make up your own list and I'll make my own. Now take those words and cross off the dis at the front of those words.

Now, let's try, just for today, to concentrate on the one word that seems to stand out above the others. Let's work on that word today in our own lives.

Let's make an honest effort to get the evil out of the way we are living our lives with regard to that one certain word.

I'll try it. You try it and let's wish each other a lot of luck in our efforts.

After all, we are fighting with a pretty powerful force in doing battle with Dis.

Try the prayer as you do battle today. Oh God, grant me the serenity... God, grant me the strength to do battle with Dis today and come out victorious. That is what I want today, God. Help me get rid of the distress in my life and to give thanks for the actual stress because stress is a sign that I am truly alive.

Focusing In

WHEN YOU ARE DOWN IN THE DUMPS IT IS DIFFICULT to see the big picture, but when you are flying high it is much easier.

Sometimes when we are flying into the Kalamazoo, Michigan Airport, when the sky is clear and we are at the right altitude, you can see the whole city there spread out before you.

When the astronauts were flying to the moon, first they saw cities below, then states, next countries and finally the world as it grew smaller and smaller.

Perhaps that is one of the reasons that they say that, in leadership roles, it is lonely at the top. I suppose there is no one there to share your exact viewpoint. No one sees the picture the same way you do because they are not really up there with you in your organization.

Lately, I have been intrigued with something called focus.

More and more businesses are changing their focus so that they can zero in on specific markets. The trend today is to become smaller in business and become the very best at what you do. Customers are demanding higher quality and excellence from their suppliers.

Quality and excellence demands greater focus. Everyone in an organization today must contribute some measure of excellence so that a product or service can compete in today's competitive global market.

When I visited a plant in North Carolina I had lunch with their general manager. I asked him if he could identify the one reason that they had become known as the safest plant in America.

"Focus." He replied. "That is what we focus on every day."

Then I asked him why one of their competitors was generally acknowledged as the number one organization when it came to quality and customer service and again he responded, "Focus."

He explained that he believed if their own people focused on quality and customer service the way they focused on safety, they could probably do as well as their competitor in that area.

Well, I forgot about our conversation for a while and then one day I received a call from the Safety Director of that competitor's firm.

They had experienced a tragic accident and, besides that, their accident rate in general left a lot to be desired.

I did a little consulting with the firm and they did a few things I suggested and then they asked me in to speak for their key safety people.

I shared with that audience what the manager of a competing manufacturer had said about focus. I congratulated them on their successful practice of focusing on quality and customer satisfaction and then I told them about something I had learned years before when I was a photographer.

I explained that when I took a picture of a nearby subject I would focus my lens so that the object was clear and sharp.

When I focused in on the nearby object, the object further away would become a blur, out of focus. And if I focused on the distant object, then the nearby object would become a blur.

Occasionally I would desire to have both objects in focus in the same picture and could try to compromise and often both objects would be out of focus. Then, as I studied photography more, I learned about something called "depth of field."

Depth of field refers to how deep your field of focus is. And you can control your depth of field by adjusting the aperture of your lens. The aperture is the diameter of the opening admitting light. The smaller the aperture, the greater the depth of field. Now light coming through a lens is like sand running through a funnel. If you want to have the right exposure of light then you must allow more time for the light to pass through a smaller hole than a larger one. The exposure takes a fraction of a second longer and you must be more knowledgeable, more professional to take such a picture, but it is possible to focus on two objects at once and produce a photograph where both objects are in sharp focus.

That is the challenge I gave that audience. To focus on safety while they continued to keep quality and customer service in sharp focus.

I explained that they would have to become more professional, they would probably have to spend more time focusing in each day, but I assured them it would be possible for them to succeed at this endeavor.

Of course, the challenge was to expand their vision without losing sight of both targets.

Evidently they were able to accept that challenge. A year later they won a national award as one of the most improved organizations in America in the field of safety.

What would be really great would be if we could have a complete set of interchangeable lenses for our lives.

Wide angle, zoom, close up, wouldn't it be great if we could keep all of the elements of our lives in sharp focus all of the time?

The truth is, when we concentrate on one thing we often have the tendency to distort a lot of the other elements of our lives.

Perhaps what we need is to make a daily effort to improve our depth of field. It might take a few more moments to accomplish things, but, just maybe, it will really improve our point of view.

Reality And Attitudes

I AM OFTEN ABOUT TWENTY YEARS BEHIND IN MY READING. Most of the books I read are found on the shelf at a local Goodwill or Salvation Army resale shop. Not that I don't buy a best seller now and then from a local bookstore, but I find that you can learn more from a book that was a best seller twenty years before and that has fallen into disfavor as the times change.

Such a book is *Winning Through Intimidation* by Robert J. Ringer. Twenty years ago I read reviews of the book, and I might have even read a chapter or two in a bookstore and decided that the philosophy was not one I would like to explore at that time.

Reading it today is a real eye opener because in a way it represents much of what went wrong in America during the seventies and the eighties. To me, Robert J. Ringer represents much of the selfishness and the "what's in it for me" approach that helped to destroy the value system in this country.

I must admit that I am discovering some really wonderful stuff in this book and I plan to apply some of it to my own philosophy in regard to selling products and ideas.

Mr. Ringer's *Theory of Sustenance of a Positive Attitude Through the Assumption of a Negative Result* is especially interesting to me.

What he is saying is that it is impossible to make a sale every time you attempt to make a sale. There are a number of unknown factors which will make it impossible for you to make a sale and these are factors over which you have absolutely no control.

In fact, you will fail to make a sale many more times than you will succeed. For that reason, he assumes that he will have a negative result. He also says that he will be prepared in every way possible to make that sale. If it is up to him then he will come through 100% with his end of the endeavor.

He has a positive attitude toward negative results and every time he fails he examines the failure to learn something.

He does everything he can possibly do to succeed, knowing he will often be defeated by those things over which he has no control. He accepts reality and goes on with a positive attitude.

When he loses he does not feel that in some way he has failed. He has succeeded in doing his best and feels that if it were not for those outside factors that he would have won.

Of course, he keeps on trying to have more control over those outside factors, but he realizes that in selling you can control only so much and some things cannot be controlled.

What about sustaining a positive attitude in everything we do through the assumption of a negative result? Could we apply this to our quest for Serenity?

I think so. What we are saying is that we will have a positive attitude, fully realizing that the reality of life is that we might often fail as much as 90% of the time when we are seeking change. And with the acceptance of that reality we can still do everything we possibly can do to succeed.

When we fail we have not really lost, we have simply endured another valuable learning experience. We examine the entire experience and draw from it precious knowledge to be used in our next attempt.

Let's face it, change is not easy. If change was that easy then there would soon be no need for it; we would have created a perfect world and a perfect life for ourselves.

So many times I have repeated the thought that it is not what happens to us in life that matters, it is how we react and how we learn from what happens that makes the difference.

Again there is that old saying that every setback is a stepping stone to progress if we make it so. Change your attitude, change your life.

God grant me the wisdom and the courage to change my attitude so that I maintain my positive attitude as I adjust to the reality of my life, Amen.

Fighting Change

WHAT DO YOU THINK OF WHEN YOU THINK OF TAIWAN? I think of those far away places with their strange sounding names.

I was in Taiwan once, I think. I'm not that sure, really. I'd given a speech in Kuala Lumpur, Malaysia, and on the way home we stopped off for a few days in Hong Kong.

Then our plane stopped somewhere out there for just a few moments; I think it was Taiwan. From there it was a stop in Seoul, Korea, Hawaii, Los Angeles, Chicago and finally the last hop to Kalamazoo, Michigan. After that, it was a twenty mile ride home. And so, when I think of Taiwan, I think of a long, long trip.

I received a letter from Taiwan last week. A publisher from Taiwan was trying to contact a friend of mine in order to purchase the rights to publish his book in the Chinese language.

I called my friend, Herb True, right away and then faxed him the letter. He asked me if I'd handle the negotiations with that firm.

I'm getting used to my Fax machine. I'd resisted buying it for years despite the fact that a dozen friends had told me that I was living in the stone ages without the benefit of a Fax.

I brushed aside their comments by telling myself that they were just a bunch of kids with new, expensive toys and that the Fax was just a fad that they would use a few times and then forget about.

My good friend, Herb True, a psychologist who teaches at Notre Dame, kept after me nearly every day until I finally purchased a Fax.

I had resisted change so well, but I eventually gave in and, when I finally purchased one, I discovered that the Fax changed the way I did business. Now I was making deals, faxing contracts and receiving them back signed, from all over the United States in just a few moments.

I had some calls from both Hawaii and Alaska, and when people wanted contracts or brochures or articles, I could supply them on that Fax in just a few seconds.

I used our Fax machine twenty-seven times last month.

I wrote a response to that publisher in Taiwan and I could just picture that letter winging its way by plane on that long, long journey to Taiwan. It would take days—weeks perhaps—and then there was the time involved for that response to return. Negotiating could take months. I looked at the letter from Taiwan once again. There was a Fax number listed. I dialed our long distance operator by hitting 00. She gave me dialing instructions and I took my letter to my Fax machine.

It was 4:50 p.m., and after sending that Fax, which took just a few seconds to complete, I went home for the night. As the Fax was being sent I had a real feeling of excitement and awe. The thought that my letter was being printed on a Fax machine at that instant in far away Taiwan was really mind boggling to me.

What a change from the days when such a correspondence would take months of dangerous travel on an ocean liner.

I was equally amazed the following morning when I arrived in my office to find a three page response from Taiwan on my Fax machine. We had a firm offer. I called Herb and then faxed the response to him. We talked it over and came up with a counter offer which I faxed immediately to Taiwan. I added that if the offer was acceptable that they should fax me a contract for signature.

Upon receipt of the signed contract they will then simply fax their bank, who will arrange for the money to be transferred to our bank. The money will be in our account that same day.

Without change, any one of the elements of this transaction could take days and weeks and months; but today, with computers and Faxes, and with people who will tune in on the tools available, wonderful things are possible.

Whenever I walk past my Fax machine I chuckle about how I fought buying that machine for over two years. It wasn't the money. It wasn't the principle of the thing either. You might call it ignorance or stupidity, but I think a better word for it would be fear. I guess I was afraid of change. I was afraid of progress and of the unknown.

We live in a world where change is a daily way of life. It is all around us. In business we learn that those people and organizations who resist change today are often doomed to failure. I've been told that I now need a modem and a laser printer for my computer. With a modem I can connect my computer with the computers of a thousand information resources. And I can team my computer up with the computers of my clients too.

And with a laser printer we can get into desktop publishing and then turn out our own books and newsletters and...

But I'm not sure that we need that stuff. Sure, some of my friends have it and they tell me it is a breakthrough and that it will save me time and increase the quality of all that we do. But, you know, those guys are like kids with new toys and they will probably just use that stuff a few times and put it away. And so I'm going to wait a while...

And besides that, it involves change . . . and deep down, I'm afraid of change.

Oh God, grant me the courage to accept change.

Wisdom

All life is that process
Of sorting out those things we cannot change
From those we must.
God, if I could just determine that
Which is changeable then
I could get on with that business
Of changing.
Wisdom, that is what I seek now, God,
That ultimate grant.
God grant me wisdom,
For wisdom will open my eyes to see
What can and what must be done.

Wisdom! Wisdom!

SOME TIME AGO I READ ABOUT A CASE WHERE a Columbia University graduate sued the school for its failure to give him wisdom. He claimed that a message carved into the mast of one of their hallowed halls on campus promised wisdom to all who entered.

Education, yes. Knowledge, yes. In fact, the young man had graduated with honors, however, in his lawsuit he charged he had received not one bit of wisdom as promised and he was suing to have all of his tuition returned to him.

The judge ruled in favor of the university stating that one could not be taught wisdom, that it must come with time and experience.

And here we are, praying to God, like Solomon once did centuries before us, for instant Wisdom as a grant, a gift.

Oh God, grant me the wisdom to know the difference between those things which I cannot change and those which I can change.

Whew! That is asking a lot. A whole lot.

I suppose that is a major reason why this must be a continuing prayer. A prayer which we utter again and again and again, day by day, twenty-four hours at a time as we seek to identify each new challenge that comes our way.

"Acceptance or courage to change? Which one is this Lord?"

"Wisdom, grant me wisdom! And God, grant me serenity, a blessed, unbounded supply of serenity which comes with acceptance."

I've just finished reading a biography of Doris Day, the singer and movie star. Don't misunderstand me, I am not recommending the book, but I look for knowledge wherever it might be found.

Doris Day's most popular recording is a song called *Que Sera, Sera*. "Whatever Will Be Will Be."

A song of resignation. Perhaps it is a song of acceptance too.

Frank Sinatra sang it another way in his song, *That's Life*.

I can't recall the words of that song but I can remember the sentiments expressed. It talks about the highs and the lows we experience each day and each month of our lives. Flying high one month and shot down the next.

And perhaps, wisdom helps us to realize that everything will not be coming up roses every day of our lives. There will be good days and good times and better days and better times, but we will also have our share of days where we are down and in the pits too. And so we pray for the serenity to accept this fact and get on with the business of making it better.

As the fellow said, "God, give me patience. And I want it NOW!"

God grant me wisdom and I certainly need it now because, quite frankly, it is not easy to know the difference between those things which I can change and those things which I cannot change, and without wisdom I seem to be spending far too much time on unchangeable things when I should be getting on with those things which, with courage, I might change.

"True wisdom is to know what is best worth knowing, and to do what is best worth doing."　　　　　　　　　　**Humphrey**

> *I am only one, but I am one;*
> *I cannot do everything*
> *But I can do something.*
> *What I can do, I ought to do*
> *And what I ought to do*
> *By the grace of God, I will do...*
> 　　　　　　　　**Canon Farrar**

Wisdom Of The Wizard

SOME DAYS I WAKE UP AND I WISH THAT I COULD walk down that yellow brick road along with Dorothy, The Tin Man, The Scarecrow and the Cowardly Lion.

We're off to see the Wizard, that wonderful Wizard of Oz.

Perhaps if you joined us you'd have your own reasons for visiting the Wizard.

Like that Cowardly Lion, I could stand for a lot more courage in my life.

My wife, Ruthie, is sick once more and I am afraid that we have run out of miracles. She's had cancer for so long and it keeps coming back and frankly, I think that Ruthie has finally just run out of the will to fight it any longer.

God, how I need courage in my life right now.

The Tin Man had no heart. There is a song in the play and movie *Damn Yankee* that says, "You've got to have heart. Miles and miles and miles of heart."

Heart is the stuff that heroes are made of. Heart gets you through the crisis each day. Heart helps you to face your troubles and come up a winner.

The Scarecrow went to the Wizard for a brain. I believe he was a lot like us. He was actually seeking wisdom.

Dorothy? Dorothy wanted to go home and yet, I think that Dorothy was seeking serenity.

And what did the Wizard give them? The Wizard gave the Cowardly Lion a medal. The Tin Man was given a testimonial watch. The Scarecrow who had no brain was given a diploma.

Now that sounds a little bit like what is happening in our education system today.

And Dorothy is told that home is where the heart is.

When the Wizard is exposed as a fraud it turns out that indeed, he really was truly wise. He taught our friends that each had greatness within and that we must all call upon our true potential to be happy and successful.

As I pray The Serenity Prayer I realize that God is not about to strike me with a divine ray of potential and bless me with new powers.

We all function at but a small portion of our true ability.

What I pray for each day is the will and the stamina and the heart to perform as I know I can and should and must.

I don't need a miracle in my life. The miracle is already inside me. What I must do is get out of the way and let it happen.

Living The Serenity Prayer

TAKE JUST A MOMENT, PLEASE, AND STUDY this drawing. How do you feel as you look at it? I found it at a garage sale and I could not resist it. It was months later when I decided to clean it up and wash the glass and polish the frame that I discovered this powerful example of The Serenity Prayer in action.

A small notice on the back of this drawing states, "Design on this note was drawn by Ann Adams, a polio patient, who prior to her illness was an artist. Through perseverance she trained herself to draw by holding a pencil between her teeth. Each original drawing takes up to two months to complete."

I put the drawing on the refrigerator at our office house and occasionally when I was feeling blue I'd take the drawing down and study it for a few moments. I'd think about this remarkable woman, Ann Adams. Then when I began to write this book, I was drawn to learn more about her life.

I made a dozen phone calls and finally a reference librarian at the Jacksonville, Florida, Library informed me that Ann had died on Mother's Day, 1992.

Thanks to newspaper clippings and the help of a few of Ann's friends, I've managed to discover how Ann Adams lived a productive, rewarding life despite her paralysis.

Ann was a beautiful, energetic, talented art student at Florida State University, age twenty-one, married with a young son, when infantile paralysis struck her. Her whole body, with the exception of some neck and mouth muscles, was totally paralyzed. Her late parents, Mr. and Mrs. J.A. Vaughan, helped take care of her during those years and the National Foundation (for Infantile Paralysis) provided the equipment and nursing services needed to keep her alive.

For the next few years, she was either in a specially designed wheelchair wearing a device that pumped air into her lungs, or in an iron lung. Mrs. J.A. Vaughan, Ann's mother, once told a reporter, "Some people look at an iron lung with awe. But I have an affection for that old thing. We like it."

All that time, Ann hoped and prayed for a recovery. Then one day a physical therapist picked up Ann's useless arm and said, "You must stop dreaming. We can't help you."

Ann explained to a reporter, "I was shattered. Cruel words can kill you. But sometimes they're more merciful because right then I lost my illusions and decided to try to draw again."

Ann said, "I discovered that you still have to accept a terrible thing even though you think doing so may kill you. After that, you have the strength to want to do something with what you have. And God has certainly given everybody something wonderful to do."

One day she heard of a male artist who was able to draw by holding a pencil in his mouth. He could breathe on his own. "I didn't know if I could emulate him or not, but I decided to try."

Ann said that it was torture. It took her ten weeks, using a pencil held between her lips, just to learn how to draw a straight line. A simple curve took her twelve weeks to master. "I found myself saying, 'Look, God, please, I'll never be able to do this alone. You are going to have to help me."

Ann struggled on. Her first drawing of a church in the woods took several months. Then later she finished four Christmas scenes. She had five hundred copies of one printed and sold them all.

Success came quickly. A year or so after she resumed her artwork, a friend made contact with a card company representative and soon Mrs. Adams' work was going out through the mail. That was the beginning of a remarkable career as a successful, professional artist.

Her sales enabled Ann to become financially self-supporting. She bought a lovely home and managed to pay for her medical expenses plus the salary of a full-time attendant. "When God closes one door, He opens another," Ann told an interviewer.

In another interview, Ann told a reporter, "Pity is for the birds, and self-pity is the most destructive thing in human life. I'm one of the happiest people you'll meet, so please don't make this a sad story."

I thought about Ann and her rewarding life. When she died at age sixty-five she had lived a productive and successful life. Despite the fact that she had to spend twelve hours each night in her iron lung for survival, plus another eight hours on a special bed where she could read books and magazines by using a special device triggered by a button under her chin to turn the pages.

The rocking motion and a mouth hose enabled her to breathe easier. Talking about her iron lung, Ann stated, "It's comfortable. It gives you a good breath, and it's enabled a lot of people like me to live because you can get a good night's rest and feel great the next day."

Still she was able to spend four hours a day in a special wheelchair outfitted with a corset containing a breathing device. She traveled, shopped at the mall and even managed vacations. And in those four hours she did her drawing. Each drawing took her hours and weeks, and yet, before she died she managed to amass a collection of several hundred original drawings.

Oh God, Grant me the serenity to accept those things I cannot change. Ann Adams' life was truly a prayer in action. After three years of hoping for the impossible, she accepted the reality of her life and went on. Calling upon God for help, she carved out her niche in history.

God, grant me the courage to change the things I can. Can you imagine the courage it took to spend ten painful weeks just learning to draw a straight line? Every time I think about Ann Adams I am in awe of her remarkable talent, but more thrilled and inspired by her courage.

God grant me the wisdom to know the difference. Take another look at that drawing of Fritz. Fritz was just one of Ann's pets. At one time she had seven dogs. Her favorite subjects were animals and Fritz was one of her favorites.

Wisdom, courage, persistence and love. That might summarize Ann's life.

Ann's son, Ken, who was just two years old when Ann was stricken with polio, is now Dr. Kenneth V. Adams, M.D., a successful cardiac care specialist.

On May 10, 1992, Ann Adams passed away. Her original art work is currently on the open market. A portion of the proceeds will be donated to charity with the remainder to pay the expenses of administering Mrs. Adams' estate and taxes.

Inquiries may be made to:

The Estate of Ann V. Adams
c/o Meryl Adams
5300 Noble Circle South
Jacksonville, FL 32211
(904) 721-8263
(904) 356-2600

by Ann Adams

Summary

S O WHAT HAVE I LEARNED FROM MY MONTHS of research and years of struggle with The Serenity Prayer? What great truths have I uncovered in my search?

How might others find greater benefits as they work with The Serenity Prayer seeking to bring greater balance and sanity to their lives?

First of all, I have discovered that The Serenity Prayer is many different things to different people. Certainly you do not need to be on a recovery program to benefit from this prayer.

Some people say the prayer in utter desperation. It is the utterance of final surrender. The prayer is the final step in admitting that the old ways of life have failed miserably and that the person saying the prayer is now ready for a change, that is, a complete change from the past.

Oh God . . . these first two words of the prayer might be cried out in complete surrender. PLEASE God. Oh Please God, listen to me.

No one else will listen to me any longer. Please God listen to me, I beg You to listen to me.

Oh God, Grant me the serenity.

For some people the prayer is a creed. A daily affirmation and a guide to living a whole, rewarding, successful life.

God, help me set my goals. Help me to learn acceptance, to live a life of acceptance of reality. And help me to find the courage to change those things in my life which can be changed.

What did I learn from this prayer? Most of all I learned that it is really difficult, if not often impossible, to sort out those things which can be changed and those things which cannot be changed regardless of how hard I try to change them.

Why is it that I spend so much of my time and effort, blindly trying again and again to change the impossible?

What many of us need is to find acceptance. If we could only accept those things we cannot change then we could devote our time and energy and our efforts to making the important changes in our lives that are possible.

When you take the time to really study this marvelous prayer it soon becomes a guide plan for living.

There seems to be no limit to the potential of this prayer. One day you discover a new dimension of the prayer, and the next day, it seems to unfold and open even greater possibilities.

Some readers take me to task for not citing Bible passages to justify my thoughts and ideas.

When I wrote my book *Love Is The Target* I started citing Bible quotes for each of the different chapters of the book. Then as I got deeper into the book I found more and more passages of the Bible that could have been cited.

Using a computer we can come up with hundreds of Bible references just on the word "Love."

What I recommend to you, the reader, is that you do your own research. Take the key words to The Serenity Prayer and find your own favorite Bible citations that give strength and meaning to The Serenity Prayer for you.

I also invite you to write down your own experiences with each of the elements of The Serenity Prayer.

Write down instances of how you have experienced a new level of Serenity in your life.

Make a list of the things you have accepted as unchangeable and how acceptance has made your life happier and your problems easier to cope with.

Spend some time making a list of the things that require change in your life. List only those things that you have decided can be changed.

Select a specific item on that list and break that challenge down into several components. Now set out to achieve that change. Make it a goal. Put a date on that goal for completion.

Make the goal realistic. See yourself already in possession of that achievement. The other necessary ingredient is work. Yes, work and persistence. Work on your goal every day.

Wow! Can you see the fantastic potential of The Serenity Prayer now? It isn't just a prayer. Sure, I believe in the power of prayer, but I am also a realist. I firmly believe in that saying, "Nothing happens until somebody does something."

Praying is great but I believe that you have to give God a little help. In fact, I believe that we have to give God a lot of help and if we just sit back and pray for miracles, we will be sadly disappointed most of the time.

So what did I really learn about The Serenity Prayer? I learned that it is a plea for sanity. It is a sincere request for clear thinking.

The Serenity Prayer is simply asking God to put the cards on the table so that we can get a better, more honest look at the hand we are playing with.

Oh God, take the smoke out of the room so that I can face my life with greater vision.

Vision, yes that is the word I have been searching for. The Serenity Prayer—A Prayer For Vision.

God, open up my eyes and let me see the way to a bright, wonderful future.

How many lives has the prayer changed? None. Can't you see the beauty of this prayer? The prayer does not call on God for a miracle. The prayer calls on God for the wisdom to know what to do and the courage to get on with the business of doing it.

The prayer didn't change people's lives. They changed their own lives and that is my challenge to you—and to myself as well.

Let's get on with it! Let's make this a better world, for ourselves and for everyone we come in contact with today.

Let's get on with the changes that are possible in our lives.

Can you see the secret that will enable us to make this prayer work?

The secret is us. We are the ones who must make it work, and with God's help we will succeed.

About The Author

ART FETTIG WAS BORN IN DETROIT, MICHIGAN JULY 5, 1929. In 1960 he moved his family to Battle Creek, Michigan, where he now resides. He married Ruthie, his wife of over thirty-eight years and she died of cancer, June 26, 1993. They have four grown children and five grandchildren.

Art Fettig began writing professionally in 1961 and he has had thirty-two books published, including *How To Hold An Audience In The Hollow Of Your Hand*, *The Three Robots* series of children's stories, *The Platinum Rule* and *Love Is The Target*.

In 1963 he began his career as a professional speaker and has made presentations in all fifty of the United States, eight Canadian Provinces and several other foreign locations including Malaysia and Hong Kong. He is now the veteran of well over 3,000 professional presentations.

Today, Art Fettig spends a great deal of time writing and making presentations in the Safety Field. His current client list includes such firms as General Motors, DuPont, Exxon, Akzo and major safety conferences and conventions throughout the world.

In 1980 he was certified as a "Speaking Professional" (C.S.P.) by the National Speakers Association.

Art continues to write and lecture on personal growth, motivation and sales, and is a frequent visitor to elementary schools where he speaks for students on "Saying yes to positive living."

Art Fettig is featured in a number of video programs on safety, and on several cassette tape programs.

During the Korean Conflict, Fettig served as a combat rifleman in the United States Army. He was wounded in combat and was awarded *The Military Order of the Purple Heart.*

For information on his availability as a professional speaker, or for a free catalog of his books and audio-visual products, please contact Growth Unlimited Inc., 36 Fairview, Battle Creek, Michigan, 49017. Phone 1-800-441-7676 or 616-965-2229. His fax number is 616-965-4522.

Growth Unlimited Catalog

JUST SAY YES -

A non-denominational, **positive value** system
for today's challenging world.

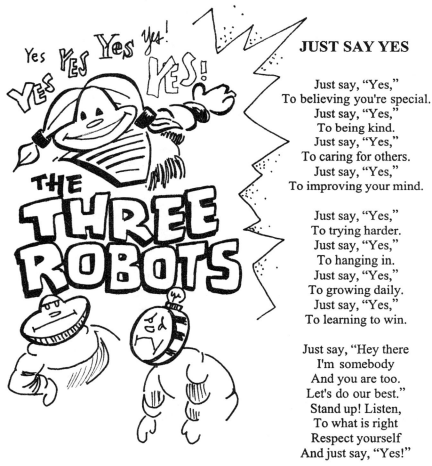

JUST SAY YES

Just say, "Yes,"
To believing you're special.
Just say, "Yes,"
To being kind.
Just say, "Yes,"
To caring for others.
Just say, "Yes,"
To improving your mind.

Just say, "Yes,"
To trying harder.
Just say, "Yes,"
To hanging in.
Just say, "Yes,"
To growing daily.
Just say, "Yes,"
To learning to win.

Just say, "Hey there
I'm somebody
And you are too.
Let's do our best."
Stand up! Listen,
To what is right
Respect yourself
And just say, "Yes!"

by Art Fettig

**The Three Robots Help Kids Say "YES"
To Positive Living**

*"Here is one of the best books I have seen to teach children
the principles of positive thinking, health and happinesss.
Art Fettig has done a charming and creative work in 'The
Three Robots' and adults will like it too. I know for I like it
tremendously."*

Dr. Norman Vincent Peale – Author of the Power of Positive Thinking

The Three Robots Just Say Yes Kit

"What a delightful book! And I love what 'Pos' does and the beautiful lesson it leaves!"

Robert Schuller – Pastor, Crystal Cathedral

2 Great Books

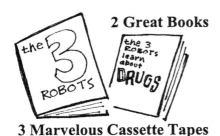

The Three Robots
Teaches how to be happy and healthy. (CHB-1)

The Three Robots Learn About Drugs
Saying "No" to drugs, "Yes" to positive living and realizing that you are "somebody special." (CHB-7)

3 Marvelous Cassette Tapes

The Three Robots–the book narrated
Your children will listen again and again. (CHT-1)

The Three Robots Learn About Drugs
An excellent narration of the book. (CHT-7)

The Just Say Yes Rap & Somebody
Features singer Paul Lee Marr. Kids love it and it reinforces positive values. (CHT-8)

1 Just Say Yes Activity Book

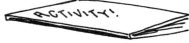

Easy to use, it gives you a ten week action program that builds self-esteem and creates life changing, positive values. (CHB-8)

10 Pos Stickers, An Achievement Card, and an "I'm a Pos" Pin

A $34.20 Value... Special – Just $29.95 (CHYK-1)

(Add $3 Shipping)

The Three Robots Books and Tapes Also Sold Individually

Books $3.95
Work Books $5.95
Tapes $5.95

Wayne Dyer:
"My children love these books. They learn positive attitudes and loving reactions to life. What greater testimonial could you ask?"

The Three Robots Just Say Yes Kit is great for parents to use in the home with their children and it can be used in classrooms too. Thousands of children have already benefited from this powerful program. Don't Delay!

> **Give your kids that rare gift of a Positive Attitude and a sense of values that will last them a lifetime.**

THE THREE ROBOTS SUCCESS KIT

Keep that positive spirit alive with your kids with more great ideas from The Three Robots!

4 More Great Books

The Three Robots Find a Grandpa
This book teaches how to become loveable, loving yourself, loving others and being loved in return. (CHB-4)

The Three Robots And The Sandstorm
Kids learn about teamwork and overcoming setbacks and disabilities. (CHB-2)

The Three Robots Discover Their Pos-Abilities
A unique 8 Step Goal Setting Process that works with people of all ages. (CHB-3)

Remembering—A book for kids to help them teach their parents to remember. Makes learning and remembering easier. (CHB-6)

The Three Robots Activity Book

More than just pictures to color, this unique collection of practical ideas helps parents and teachers focus the child's energy on life changing, positive values. (CHB-5)

10 Pos Stickers, an Achievement Card and an "I'm a Pos" pin

Four Fantastic Tapes

You receive cassette tape narrations of all four of the above great books. Kids listen to the tape again and again, reinforcing these powerful, concepts in their subconscious minds. Helps to overcome the bombardment of negativism they are exposed to daily. (CHT-2-3-4-6)

Everything Above! A $48.05 Value Now Just $39.95! (CHSK-1)

Why wait until your children are grown up and accidentally stumble upon success concepts? Teach them now about success and happiness. As a bonus you will learn these powerful success principles as you share them with your children.

> *"The Three Robots is a story for kids—but adults need the message too. It's simple, clear, direct, motivational and much needed in our society. I believe it will help kids of all ages."*
> Zig Ziglar, the World's #1 Motivation Speaker

the POS PARENTING Package

"Art Fettig, in his new book The Three Robots, is filling a great need. Many young children blame a 'bad day' on a parent or teacher—even the weather! To teach children that no one can give them happiness and that they will determine whether they have a happy or a sad day, is to teach them one of the most important lessons in life."

Marilyn VanDerbur – Noted educator and former Miss America

2 Great Books

Pos Parenting – A guide to greatness, with 25 keys for building your child's positive self-esteeem. In America today we are experiencing an epidemic of low self-esteem. The symptoms are evident everywhere. Low school grades, lack of friendships, TV addiction, drug abuse, promiscuity; yes, even the highest teenage suicide rate in the world. This book addresses the problem and offers suggestions on how you can build not only your child's self-esteem but your own as well. (PRB-1)

It Only Hurts When I Frown – A series of humorous-serious sketches on family relations and on the joy of raising 4 children. Hilarious, real and heart touching. It will make you laugh and nod your head and say, "Yes, I've been there too." (PRB-2)

A Stirring 2 Tape Audio Program

Positive Parenting. Taped live for an audience of concerned parents. You'll discover that you are not alone and that raising children today takes a special person with a special commitment. You'll laugh and no doubt you will cry, but most important, you will probably do a better job of parenting after hearing this touching program. (PRA-1)

A $33.90 Value – Special Just $29.95 (PRC-1)

84

Fantastic Combination Offer
Get All Three Combinations At A Remarkable Savings

Yes, we'd like you to benefit from all of our products created for parents and children. You receive all three combinations, The Three Robot Just Say Yes Kit (a $34.20 value), The Three Robot Success Course (a $48.05 value), and the Pos Parenting Package (a $33.90 value), **a total retail value of $116.16, all for just $79.95**, plus $5 shipping. (PRC-2)

When you buy the complete package we will include an attractive vinyl 8-pack album for the tapes.

Unfortunately, today, most people learn about success and happiness in some form of rehabiliation program, that is, if they survive.

The question you must ask yourself is this, "Do I want my children to learn that they are special, wonderful, unique individuals now or do I want them to discover it after they have really made a mess of their lives?"

This valuable combination of great life changing ideas and techniques are yours just for the asking at a price that anyone can afford.

Just call us at 1-800-441-7676 right now and get started immediately on a success program that will not only touch your child's life but yours as well.

To order just call us, or if you prefer you can send your check or money order to Growth Unlimited Inc., 36 Fairview, Battle Creek, Michigan, 49017. Our FAX Number is 616-965-4522. Yes, we take Visa, Master Card or American Express.

Call us at 1-800-441-7676 Today!

A $116.16 Value – Special Just $79.95   (PRC-2)

(Add $5 Shipping)

"It captures the world of childhood imagination beautifully"
Art Linkletter, author of Kids Say the Darndest Things

The Platinum Rule —— The age old secret to happiness and prosperity

"It is terrific!" – *W. Clement Stone*   "Wonderful message" – *Og Mandino*

"The Platinum Rule is great. And it's needed too" – *Dr. Norman Viucent Peale*

Paperback Edition   (PDB-3) $5.95
Special Hardcover Autographed Edition   (PDB-3H) $12.95
Please add $3 shipping

Love is the Target —— An answer for troubled Americans, today

This little book will provide you with the answer you seek to live a happier, healthier, more productive life.

Paperback   (LTB) $5.95

Now available on video and audio tape.
Taped live with a great audience, this 44 minute presentation will entertain and inspire you.

Audio Tape   (LTT) $9.95
Video Tape   (LTV) $39.95

A $51.85 Value	*Super Special* – Get all three!
Just $40!	*The book, the audio and the* *video tapes for just (LTC) $40.00*

Serenity! Serenity!—Living The Serenity Prayer

One man's quest for serenity, acceptance and courage.

Paperback (SSB)   *$5.95*

Coming Soon

Audio and Video Tapes of both The Platinum Rule and Serenity! Serenity! To be recorded with a live audience, Art Fettig's presentations have the fire and the passion that will reach you and touch your life. Call or write for information from Growth Unlimited Inc., 36 Fairview, Battle Creek, MI, 49017.   Call 1-800-441-7676!

Art Fettig is accepting a limited number of speaking engagements to help spread the powerful message contained in his book Love is the Target. For more information on rates and availability call 1-800-441-7676.

How to Hold an Audience in the Hollow of Your Hand

Art Fettig, veteran of nearly 4,000 professional speeches reveals the techniques of the top professionals. 7 powerful ways to win an audience in the first 5 minutes and 11 techniques to keep them listening. A proven winner. (PSB-1, $9.95)

Anatomy of a Speech

Discover how to create exciting, powerful, winning speeches using the vignette style of speech construction. Save hours and improve your presentations immediately. (PSBK-1, $3.95)

The Art of Public Speaking

Learn to use humor effectively. How to win an audience, how to stack the odds in your favor. Proven techniques demonstrated by top professional speakers, recorded at live presentations. 4-Tape Album,.(PSA-1, $49.95)

The Best Verse of Art Fettig and Friends

Camera ready copy of Art Fettig's most popular verses. Includes Growth, Self-Esteem Credo, Just Say Yes, Teacher-Teacher, My Brother Joe and many others. (BV-1, $3.95)

Selling Lucky

By applying the sensational sales methods revealed in this book, you'll achieve more in your business, job or personal relationships. A no-holds barred look at what it takes to be a great salesperson. (SLB-1, $9.95)

Selling Luckier Yet

This companion volume to "Selling Lucky" is full of interesting anecdotes, personal sales strategies and many new ways to close that sale. (SLB-2, $5.95)

Mentor: Secret of the Ages

Now, you'll be introduced to your own personal mentor, your "friend in need" in time of crisis. Whenever you want, you'll be able to turn to this written masterpiece for guidance and comfort. Hardcover (PDB-1, $9.95), Cassette (PDT-1, $9.95) or both (PDC-1, $15.95)

The Art of Greatness

Unlock the "success consciousness" that lies deep within you. This program gives you the golden key. A 2-tape album filled with all the timeless methods you'll need. (PDA-2, $19.95)

The Speaker's Bonus Special

Here's what you get:

The Art of Public Speaking 4-tape album
How to Hold an Audience in the Hollow of Your Hand Book
Anatomy of a Speech Booklet
How Funny Are You? Book
The Art of Greatness 2-tape album

A $89.75 Value for Only $59.95   (PSC-1)

GROWTH UNLIMITED, INC.
36 Fairview
Battle Creek, MI 49017
Toll Free 1-800-441-7676
616-965-2229   Fax: 616-965-4522

ACT TODAY FOR YOUR CHILD'S FUTURE

Item No.	Description	Quantity	Price Each	Price Total
			Subtotal	
			MI Res, 4% Tax	
			+ 10% Shipping ($3 Minimum)	
	Please find my check or money order enclosed		**Total Order**	

Charge my VISA ❑   **MasterCard** ❑   **or American Express** ❑

Card No:		Expires (Mo/Yr):
Signature:		Tel. No:
Name:		
Address:		
City:	St:	Zip:

We guarantee 100% satisfaction on all of our products. If, for any reason, you are not delighted with any of our products, just return them for a 100% refund.

SEND IN YOUR ORDER TODAY!